♛ Contents

Henry's England

When Henry was king, most people lived in small villages in the countryside. Many worked on farms owned by rich people. Life was difficult.

Sheep farmers working in the fields at the time when Henry was king.

4

Rich people lived in big houses. They wore expensive clothes and ate huge meals. Servants cooked for them and musicians entertained them.

Rich guests enjoy a wedding party in a village close to London.

5

Henry becomes king

Henry Tudor was born in 1491. He became king in 1509 when he was 17 years old. He was tall and handsome.

A painting of Henry when he became king of England.

Henry is famous for having six wives. He wanted a son to rule England after him.

These paintings show Henry's six wives.

Catherine of Aragon

Anne Boleyn

Jane Seymour

Anne of Cleves

Catherine Howard

Catherine Parr

The first and second wives

Henry's first wife was Catherine of Aragon. She didn't have a boy, so Henry divorced her. Then he married Anne Boleyn.

These actors have dressed up as Henry and Catherine.

Anne Boleyn had a daughter who later became Queen Elizabeth I, but she did not have a son. Henry stopped loving her. Anne was beheaded.

Henry was married to Anne Boleyn for three years.

The third and fourth wives

Henry's third wife was Jane Seymour. Henry loved her the most. She died soon after giving birth to a son, Edward.

This painting shows Henry VIII with his third wife, Jane.

Henry's fourth wife was Anne of Cleves. He was not happy with her so he divorced her after six months.

Henry gave Hever Castle to Anne of Cleves when they had divorced.

The fifth and sixth wives

Henry's fifth wife was Catherine Howard. She was beheaded after Henry found out she had lots of boyfriends.

Catherine Howard was kept in the Tower of London before she was beheaded.

Henry's sixth and last wife was
Catherine Parr. Henry was ill and
Catherine looked after him during
the last few years of his life.

After Henry died,
Catherine married
Jane Seymour's
brother, Thomas.

Sports and hobbies

Henry was a great athlete when he was young. He loved to ride horses. He went hunting and enjoyed jousting.

These riders are showing people what jousts looked like.

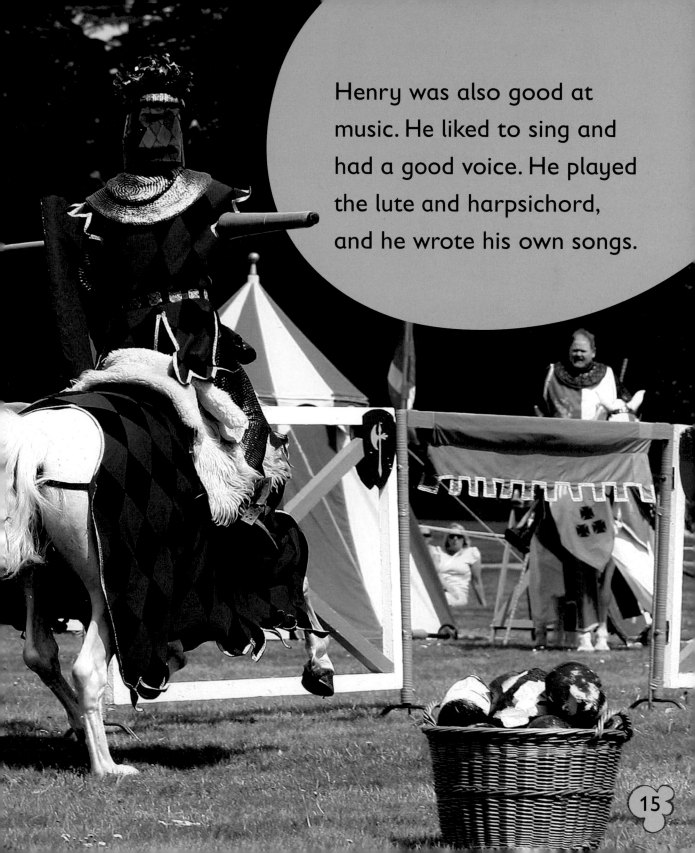

Henry was also good at music. He liked to sing and had a good voice. He played the lute and harpsichord, and he wrote his own songs.

Houses and castles

Henry wanted to keep
England safe from its enemies.
So he built lots of castles.

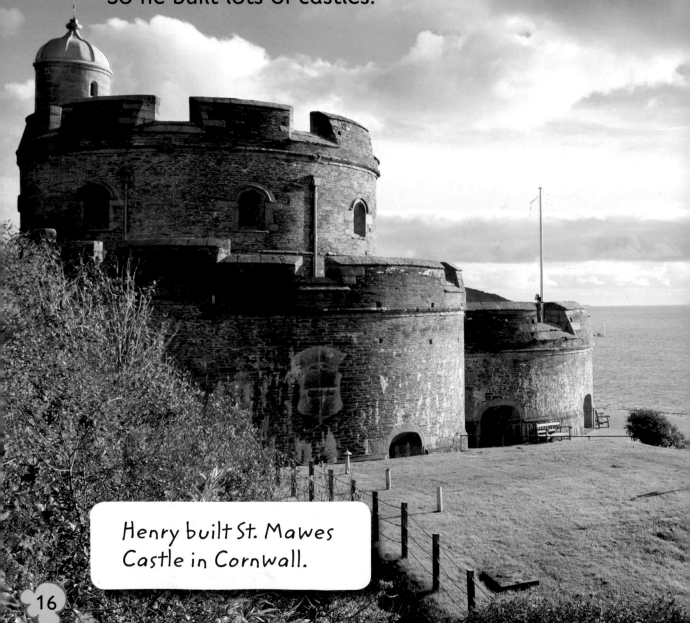

Henry built St. Mawes
Castle in Cornwall.

Henry often travelled round England to meet his people. When he was in London, he liked to live at Hampton Court Palace.

You can visit Hampton Court Palace today and see where Henry lived.

There is a story that the ghost of Catherine Howard haunts Hampton Court Palace!

👑 The *Mary Rose*

Henry had lots of warships built.

His favourite ship was the *Mary Rose*.

In 1545, Henry watched it set sail.

Disaster struck — the ship sank!

700 people crowded onto the *Mary Rose*. It was meant to hold 400.

We know what the *Mary Rose* looked like because people drew pictures of it at the time.

No one knows for sure why the *Mary Rose* sank. In **1982**, the ship was brought up from the bottom of the sea. You can visit it today in Portsmouth, England.

Some of the objects found on the *Mary Rose*.

comb

mug

bowls

The end of Henry's life

Henry was fat and cross when he was old. Look at the picture below and the picture on page 6. They don't look like the same person!

Henry died in 1547. His only son, Edward, became King Edward VI when he was 9. He died when he was 15.

A suit of armour worn by Henry VIII when he was a strong young man.

Henry's six wives: a quiz!

On this page, you can see pictures of Henry's six wives. There is a little rhyme about what happened to each of them:

> *Divorced, beheaded, died,*
> *Divorced, beheaded, survived!*

If you read through the book again, you'll be able to find out what happened to each wife. The answers are at the bottom of the page.

Anne Boleyn

Catherine Howard

Anne of Cleves

Catherine Parr

Catherine of Aragon

Jane Seymour

22

Answers: Catherine of Aragon – divorced; Anne Boleyn – beheaded; Jane Seymour – died;
Anne of Cleves – divorced; Catherine Howard – beheaded; Catherine Parr – survived

Make a yeoman's pudding

Tudors ate simple bread to fill their stomachs. A yeoman was a hard-working farmer. Ask an adult to help you make this yeoman's pudding so you can taste what Tudors ate!

You will need:
• 2-3 slices of rough-grained brown bread
• a dash of milk • a knob of butter • 2 eggs
• 1 tbsp of honey
• a pinch of nutmeg

1. Cut the bread into small chunks. Beat the eggs, honey and nutmeg together in a bowl. Add a little milk and stir.

2. Melt the butter in a frying pan. Dip the bread into the egg and milk mixture and place in the pan.

3. Pour the rest of the mixture over the bread in the pan. When it's cooked, cut into slices and eat – yummy!

Glossary

armour metal clothes that soldiers wore in battles long ago

athlete someone who does sports in which people run, jump, and throw things

beheaded to have your head cut off

divorce when two people divorce they end their marriage

enemies people who want to fight against you

entertain to entertain people means to do things that they enjoy watching, or things that make them laugh.

expensive something that is expensive costs a lot of money

harpsichord a musical instrument that looks and sounds like a piano

jousting a sport where horsemen try to knock each other off their horses

lute a musical instrument that looks and sounds a bit like a guitar

Index